W9-DEV-432

11-1-19
$24.95
11/19

Oceans

THE WORLD'S BIOMES

Deserts

Grasslands

Oceans

Rainforests

Wetlands

THE WORLD'S BIOMES

Oceans

Kimberly Sidabras

Mason Crest
Philadelphia

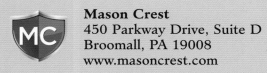

Mason Crest
450 Parkway Drive, Suite D
Broomall, PA 19008
www.masoncrest.com

Printed and bound in the United States of America.

CPSIA Compliance Information: Batch #B2018.
For further information, contact Mason Crest at 1-866-MCP-Book.

First printing
1 3 5 7 9 8 6 4 2

Library of Congress Cataloging-in-Publication Data

 Names: Sidabras, Kimberly, author.
 Title: Oceans / Kimberly Sidabras.
 Description: Philadelphia : Mason Crest Publishers, 2019. | Series: The
  world's biomes | Includes bibliographical references and index. |
  Audience: Age 12. | Audience: Grade 7 to 8.
 Identifiers: LCCN 2017048386| ISBN 9781422240380 (hardcover) | ISBN
  9781422277539 (ebook)
 Subjects: LCSH: Ocean—Juvenile literature. | Marine ecology—Juvenile
  literature.
 Classification: LCC GC21.5 .S53 2019 | DDC 577.7—dc23
 LC record available at https://lccn.loc.gov/2017048386

THE WORLD'S BIOMES series ISBN: 978-1-4222-3794-6

QR CODES AND LINKS TO THIRD-PARTY CONTENT

Table of Contents

KEY ICONS TO LOOK FOR:

Words to understand: These words with their easy-to-understand definitions will increase the reader's understanding of the text while building vocabulary skills.

Sidebars: This boxed material within the main text allows readers to build knowledge, gain insights, explore possibilities, and broaden their perspectives by weaving together additional information to provide realistic and holistic perspectives.

Educational Videos: Readers can view videos by scanning our QR codes, providing them with additional educational content to supplement the text. Examples include news coverage, moments in history, speeches, iconic sports moments and much more!

Text-dependent questions: These questions send the reader back to the text for more careful attention to the evidence presented there.

Research projects: Readers are pointed toward areas of further inquiry connected to each chapter. Suggestions are provided for projects that encourage deeper research and analysis.

Series glossary of key terms: This back-of-the-book glossary contains terminology used throughout this series. Words found here increase the reader's ability to read and comprehend higher-level books and articles in this field.

 Words to Understand

basalt—a heavy, dark rock that forms the floors of the oceans, and some oceanic islands such as the Galápagos, Hawaii, and Iceland.

continent—a slab of relatively light rock that "floats" on the heavier rock of the Earth's mantle. The Earth has seven continents: Africa, Antarctica, Asia, Australia/Oceania, Europe, North America, and South America.

current—a large-scale movement of ocean water caused by heating and cooling combined with the rotation of the Earth.

mantle—the thick layer of heavy rock that lies beneath the Earth's crust, and forms most of the volume of the Earth.

mid-ocean ridge—a double chain of underwater mountains that extends along a rift in the ocean floor. New ocean floor is created at mid-ocean ridges, as the Earth's crust on each side is pulled apart.

minerals—the natural materials that make up rocks. They are carried in ocean water, and many are used as nutrients by the tiny plants of the plankton.

ocean floor—the bed of the deep ocean, beyond the continental shelves. It is made of basalt covered with fine silt, or "ooze."

tide—a movement of water from one place to another caused by the gravity of the Moon, and modified by the gravity of the Sun. Makes the water level rise and fall, and causes local water flows called tidal streams.

trench—a deep rift in the ocean floor, created when oceanic crust is dragged down into the mantle rock by movements within the Earth.

The continents and islands of the Earth are dwarfed by the vastness of its oceans, which cover about 71 percent of the Earth's surface.

What Are Oceans?

A visitor from space approaching the Earth from above Hawaii in the Pacific Ocean would see a blue planet, because the Pacific covers almost half the world. It is bigger than all the *continents* put together—a vast expanse of water extending from Alaska to the fringes of Antarctica. In addition to the Pacific, scientists have identified four other deep oceans—the Atlantic Ocean, the Arctic Ocean, the Indian Ocean, and the ice-bound Southern Ocean that surrounds Antarctica. However, these five major oceans of the earth are in reality one large interconnected water body.

Many people use the terms "ocean" and "sea" interchangeably when speaking about the ocean. However, there is a geographical difference between those two terms. Seas are smaller and shallower than oceans, and are usually located where the land and ocean meet. Typically, seas are partially enclosed by land. Most are part of a larger ocean—for example, the

Caribbean Sea and the Gulf of Mexico are both part of the Atlantic Ocean, while the Bering Sea is part of the Pacific. The largest of the seas (the Mediterranean Sea) is about one-fifth the size of the smallest of the oceans (the Arctic).

Together, the deep oceans and seas cover about 71 percent of the Earth's surface, and make up by far the largest biome on the planet. Formed by the titanic geological forces that have shaped the continents, their waters conceal dramatic submarine landscapes of deep *trenches*, high mountains, and active volcanoes.

Oceans are not just broad puddles on the surface of the Earth. Their average depth is more than 2 miles (3.5 kilometers), while the average height of the land above sea level is just 3,280 feet (1,000 meters). In some places, underwater trenches plunge to depths of 6 miles (10 km) or more; such trenches could swallow Mount Everest

Biome versus Ecosystem

A biome is a very large ecological area, with plants and animals that are adapted to the environmental conditions there. Biomes are usually defined by physical characteristics—such as climate, geology, or vegetation—rather than by the animals that live there. For example, deserts, rainforests, and grasslands are all examples of biomes. Plants and animals within the biome have all evolved special adaptations that make it possible for them to live in that area.

A biome is not quite the same as an ecosystem, although they function in a similar way. An ecosystem is formed by the interaction of living organisms within their environment. Many different ecosystems can be found within a single biome. Components of most ecosystems include water, air, sunlight, soil, plants, microorganisms, insects, and animals. Ecosystems exist on land and in water, with sizes ranging from a small puddle to an enormous swath of desert.

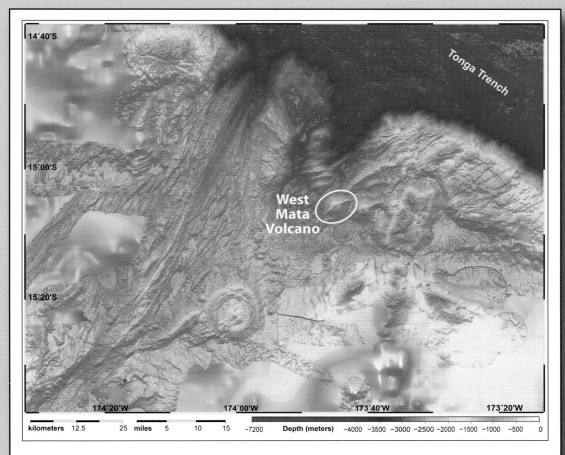

This sonar-created map of the ocean floor shows deep trenches, plateaus, and volcanic mountains in the western Pacific Ocean, an area of intense volcanic activity.

with almost a mile to spare. The sheer volume of water in the world's oceans is enormous—it has been estimated at over 240 million cubic miles (a billion km³).

The Active Ocean Floor

The *ocean floor* is made from a special kind of rock, called *basalt*. It is very heavy and black, and quite different from the

Lava flows from one of the five volcanos that make up the Big Island of Hawaii, eventually reaching the Pacific Ocean. The lava cools rapidly as it reaches the water and forms solid rock, which over time builds up the volcanic island.

rock that forms continents.

If you could cut the Earth in half, it would look a bit like the inside of a giant peach. On the outside is a thin crust, like the peach skin—except that the Earth's crust is not one continuous piece but is instead made up of several enormous pieces, called plates. Below the crust is a very thick layer of dense, heavy, hot rock called the *mantle*, which is like the flesh of a peach. At the center of the Earth is the "peach pit"—a core of metallic iron and nickel.

The core of the Earth is like a vast nuclear reactor. It generates huge amounts of heat, which makes the rock of the mantle extremely hot. The mantle rock is a lot hotter than the lava that pours from volcanoes, but it stays solid because it is under pressure due to the huge weight of rock above it. This raises the melting point of the mantle rock and stops it from becoming liquid. Yet, despite this, the mantle rock can flow sluggishly, like soft clay.

As heat diffuses from the Earth's core, it generates convection *currents*, just like the currents you see churning through a pan of boiling soup on the kitchen stove. And just as the soup boils up and around, so the mantle rock surges up toward the cool, hard crust of the Earth. As it moves away from the core, the mantle rock spreads out, cools, and sinks again.

Basalt is formed from molten *minerals* that boil up from the mantle. The basalt of the ocean floor is lighter than mantle

Where Did Earth's Water Come From?

As the Earth was cooling down after its formation 4.6 billion years ago, huge clouds of volcanic gases poured from its interior. These included vast amounts of water vapor that eventually cooled and condensed to form the oceans.

The volcanic gases also included chlorine—the gas that gives public swimming pools their peculiar smell. The chlorine was dissolved in the early oceans, and it is possible that they smelled a bit like swimming pools. Overtime, however, rivers pouring off the continents picked up other substances from the rocks and carried them into the oceans. These included sodium, a metal that reacts chemically with chlorine to produce sodium chloride, or salt. It is sodium chloride that gives ocean water its distinctive salty taste.

Educational Video

For an overview of life in the ocean around Antarctica, scan here:

rock, so it lies on top of the mantle like a layer of oil on water.

The rock that forms continents is lighter than basalt, so the continents "float" higher on the mantle than the rock that makes up the ocean floor. In some places, such as along the edges of the Atlantic Ocean, the ocean floor and the continental rock are locked together. But in other places, such as the Pacific coast of South America, the heavy basalt of the ocean floor is constantly being dragged beneath the lighter continental rock by movements within the Earth. The tectonic plates that make-up the Earth's crust move very slowly, at just an inch a year, but as they move, they drag the ocean floors with them.

In places where the mantle rock is cooling and sinking, it drags the ocean floor rock that rests on top of it down into the Earth. This creates deep ocean trenches like the 7 mile (11 km) Marianas Trench in the western Pacific. As the rocks grind their way downward, the friction causes volcanoes to erupt along the edges of the trenches. The volcanoes in Japan, Java, and the Andes mountains of South America were formed in this way.

As they are pulled down at the edges, the great plates of oceanic crust move apart to form immense rifts in mid-ocean. As these rifts open, the pressure on the hot rock below is released, so it melts. Molten rock squirts up into the cold ocean

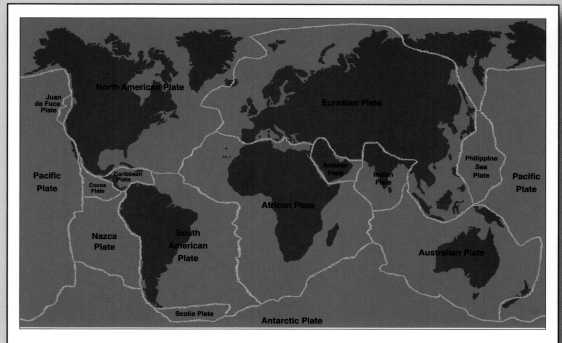

World map showing the tectonic plates that make up the Earth's crust. The place where the Eurasian and African plates meet the North and South American plates is known as the Mid-Atlantic Ridge. Earthquakes and volcanic activity are common in the places where tectonic plates meet.

water and solidifies to form submarine mountain chains called *mid-ocean ridges*.

The longest of these, the Mid-Atlantic Ridge, is 43,500 miles (70,000 km) long, running from Spitzbergen in the Arctic almost to Antarctica. The two sides of the ridge are steadily moving apart, and this is pushing the Americas away from Europe and Africa. The same thing is happening to the Red Sea between North Africa and the Middle East, which is getting one inch wider every year. In a hundred million years' time, the Red Sea could be an ocean as big as the Atlantic.

Breaking waves pound at solid rock, splitting it into boulders and gradually reducing it to small stones and beach sand.

Currents and Water Movement

The waters of the world's oceans are kept in constant motion by powerful currents that sweep across the globe. Driven by a combination of solar heat, the rotation of the Earth, and ocean winds, these currents have a huge influence on global weather systems and climate, for better or worse.

Ocean water is continually on the move. Some ocean currents carry water around the ocean surface, while others move water down into the depths, across the ocean floor, and up again. These surface and deep-water currents interact in a complex pattern.

Currents are driven by a combination of forces, including the temperature of the water. Close to the poles, the ocean water is extremely cold—cold enough to freeze at the surface. Since sea ice is pure water, the cold water beneath the ice becomes more salty and dense, and sinks to the bottom. In the north Atlantic this cold "bottom water" flows south toward the tropics, while at the surface, warmer water flows in from the Gulf of Mexico. The warm surface current is known as the Gulf Stream. It is the Gulf Stream that gives northern Europe its mild climate.

Ocean currents are also driven by the turning of the Earth. The rotation creates huge circular currents, called eddies, at the surface. In the northern hemisphere, these currents move clockwise. They flow westward along the Equator, alongside similar currents that swirl counterclockwise in the southern hemisphere.

The movement of these huge masses of water from the tropics toward the poles and back again has a powerful effect on air temperatures above the oceans. Warm water carried toward the poles warms up the air above, making the climate milder. Warm air rises, and this causes low pressure zones that suck in air from areas where colder water is cooling the air and making it sink. The moving air masses create winds that blow across the oceans, and these then help drive the currents. So the winds and currents are intimately connected, and the world's weather is partly controlled by the movements of the oceans.

El Niño and La Niña

One of the most powerful ocean currents is the Humboldt

Current, which sweeps up the western coast of South America, carrying cold water from Antarctica. At the Equator, it turns west past the Galápagos Islands and out into the Pacific Ocean. The cold waters of the Humboldt Current are rich in microscopic food, which supports much of the wildlife in the region. But each December, the current gets weaker as the strong winds that drive it ease off. This allows warmer water, very poor in food, to flow in from the north. This seasonal effect is called El Niño. It usually lasts for four to six weeks, but every few years, it can last for up to nine months, wiping out the food supply in the region. Fish vanish, seabirds starve, and the warm water disrupts the climate, causing droughts and coastal flooding throughout the tropics.

The opposite of a strong El Niño year is known as La Niña. During a La Niña period, the Pacific Ocean has cooler-than-usual temperatures at the Equator. A La Niña period often, but not always, follows a strong El Niño period.

In the United States, the impacts of El Niño and La Niña can be most clearly seen during wintertime. During El Niño years, winter temperatures are warmer than normal in the Midwestern states, and cooler than normal in the Southern states. During a La Niña year, winter temperatures are generally warmer than normal in the Southeast and cooler than normal in the Northwest.

Waves and Tides

The wind also heaps up the waves that roll across the oceans. Waves are ripples on the ocean surface, like the ripples on the surface of a pond. Yet the weight of water in a wave can be colossal, and when it reaches the coast and breaks, toppling forward to crash on the shore, all that weight is turned into destructive power. Waves smash and grind at coastal rocks, breaking them slowly into tiny pieces, then sweeping away the pieces and piling them up as beaches and banks.

The Moon also affects the oceans. The Moon's gravity pulls on the water of the oceans as the Moon orbits the Earth. This causes the daily rise and fall of the *tides*. It also causes "tidal streams"—horizontal movements of water associated with the rise and fall of the tide. In places, these tidal effects can cause powerful local currents that can transform calm coastal waters into ferocious torrents and whirlpools, much more dangerous than the great waves of the open ocean.

Text-Dependent Questions

1. What is the difference between an ocean and a sea?
2. What sort of rock makes up the ocean floor? How is it formed?
3. What is the Mid-Atlantic Ridge?

Research Project

Select one of the five major oceans. Using your school library or the internet, do some research. Where is this ocean located, and what are some of the animals or plants that are found only there? Write a two-page report that details your findings and present it to your class.

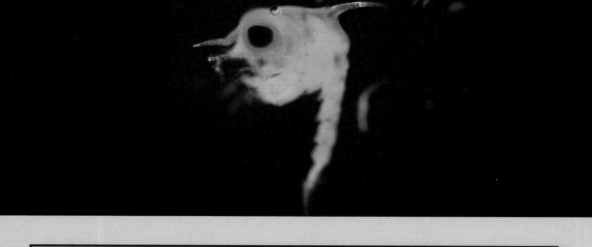

Words to Understand

continental shelf—the submerged fringe of a continent, covered with sea water to a depth of less than 1,300 feet (400 meters).

coral reef—a ridge of limestone rock built up from the stony "skeletons" of anemonelike sea creatures called corals.

mangrove—a kind of tree that grows in coastal mudflats, forming forests or mangrove swamps.

nutrients—any substances used by living things to build their bodies or turn into energy, but especially the minerals used by plants and oceanic plankton.

plankton—the living things, mostly microscopic, that drift in the ocean. Includes tiny plants called phytoplankton, which can make food using the energy of the Sun, and floating animals called zooplankton.

scuba diver—a human diver using an oxygen tank and breathing apparatus. The word "scuba" is made up of the initial letters of Self-Contained Underwater Breathing Apparatus.

sea-grass—a flowering plant that grows in shallow sea water, resembling grass.

Plankton is a term used for microscopic green plants and tiny animals, which all drift in the sunlit surface layers of the ocean. The small crab larvae shown in this magnified photograph are a type of plankton.

Life in the Oceans

The oceans contain the biggest, most bloodthirsty killers on Earth, refined by evolution into marvels of speed and efficiency. But these spectacular hunters are just part of a huge and complex web of life that relies for its survival on clouds of microscopic floating plants and animals known as *plankton*.

All land animals depend on plants for their survival, and ocean animals are the same. Even the killer sharks that prowl tropical seas rely on plant life, because they prey on fish that have eaten smaller animals, which in turn have fed on plankton. This kind of feeding relationship is called a food chain—and in the ocean, all food chains lead to plankton.

The microscopic green plants are the first and most important link in the chain, because they can turn raw chemicals into the proteins and carbohydrates that animals use as food. Tiny animals are part of the plankton too, feeding on the microscopic plants. Many of these animals are little bigger than the plants they eat. They include great swarms of shrimplike animals called krill, smaller creatures called copepods, and the tiny, floating larvae of animals such as crabs, barnacles, mussels, clams, starfish, and sea urchins. All of these plankton animals are too small to swim against the ocean currents, and so they drift where the currents take them. Krill and copepods spend their whole lives adrift, while other planktonic animals only drift until they turn into adults.

The Value of Plankton

In plankton-rich areas like the ocean waters off western South America, the plankton swarms attract schools of small fish such as anchovies, sardines, and herring. Many of them feed by straining water through their gills to trap the plankton. Bigger plankton eaters like the enormous basking shark use exactly the same method of feeding.

The even-larger baleen whales have their own way of harvesting plankton. They surge through swarms of plankton such as krill, taking great gulps of water. Then they use their tongues to push the water out through the curtains of bristly baleen that fringe their enormous mouths, and the krill are trapped on the bristles.

Schools of small plankton-feeding fish such as herring are the main targets of larger hunters like tuna, marlin, sailfish, small sharks, and dolphins. Many of these are built for speed, with massive muscles and superb streamlining. A sailfish, for example, can outswim a speedboat and accelerate to speeds of 81 mph (130 kph) or more as it closes in on its prey.

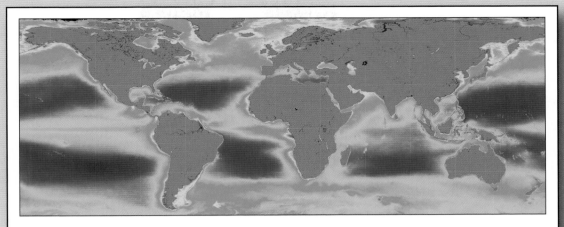

This satellite image shows amounts of plankton in the oceans. The pale green areas of the oceans have the most plankton, while the darkest blue areas are "marine deserts" with no plankton.

Sailfish hunt alone, but tuna and dolphins hunt in packs. When they find a school of food fish such as herring, they surge at them in a group attack. The herring defend themselves by forming a tight, swirling ball of fast-swimming fish. The hunters try to break up the ball, so that they can pick off the fish one by one. Dolphins use pulses of sound and bursts of bubbles to confuse the school, and often succeed in scattering and eating them all. Tuna are almost as efficient, surrounding the school and diving in and out to snap up their victims in a feeding frenzy.

As the undersea hunters attack these swirling balls of fish from below, they often drive them toward the surface. Here, they may be targeted by ocean birds such as albatrosses, brown pelicans, gannets, and auks, which dive into the water to seize the smaller fish in their bills.

The commotion of these attacks, and even the taste of blood

in the water, can be sensed from far away. It alerts the most powerful predators of all—the orcas, or killer whales, and the large sharks like the great white and tiger sharks. These formidable killers target the tuna and dolphins for their meals, rather than the schools of small fish.

Life at the Ocean's Edge

The shallow fringes of the world's oceans are the richest of all marine habitats. The fertile, sunlit waters are often thick with plant life, and this supports a huge variety of animals. Many swim freely in the water, but many more stay anchored in one place for life, filtering their food from the water.

In some parts of the world, such as volcanic islands, the deep ocean begins just offshore. But most continents have been so worn away at the fringes by the constant battering of the waves that their real edges are now underwater, several miles from the coast. The seabed slopes gently from the coast to this true continental edge, where it plunges into the depths. The region between the coast and the continental edge is called the *continental shelf*.

The waters of the continental shelves are among the richest habitats in the oceans. This is mainly because they are quite shallow. The seabed is rarely more than 590 feet (180m) beneath the surface, so it lies within the zone of water that is

Educational Video

Scan here for a video on plankton and its importance to healthy oceans:

Off the Pacific coast of North America, thick forests of kelp, a type of seaweed, swarm with food for animals such as seals and sea otters.

lit up by the sun. Close inshore, the light allows seaweed to grow on the bottom, where it shelters all kinds of animals. The water itself is often thick with plankton, which thrives on the mineral *nutrients* swept in from the deep ocean and flowing into the sea from rivers. The drifting clouds of plankton feed a huge variety of other animals.

Since they are surrounded by floating food, many continental shelf animals stay in one place and allow their meals to come to them. Mussels root themselves to rocks, and feed by sucking water through their bodies and filtering out the plankton. Sea anemones catch tiny animals using tentacles armed with stinging cells. Many marine worms live in tubes, and extend feathery fans to snare the floating plankton. And rocks, wrecks, and even large strands of seaweed are encrusted with colonies of sea squirts, sea mats, corals, and other plantlike animals, all of which feed on the plankton in the water.

The stay-at-home animals are attacked and eaten by more mobile creatures such as starfish and sea urchins. Creatures such as crabs and sea snails are scavengers, living on scraps. Predators such as the octopus come out at dawn and dusk to hunt crabs and snails. Their excellent camouflage enables them to blend into their surroundings, and they grab passing prey with their long arms. Flatfish and rays cruise sandy areas searching for tubeworms and half-buried shellfish. They are then eaten by big fish such as conger eels and coastal sharks.

Tidal Shores and Coral Reefs

The richest coastal waters are often the shallowest, since these get the most light. But close inshore, the water drains away twice a day as the tide goes out. Few sea creatures can cope with this, but since there is so much food in the water, any animals that can survive exposure to the air can live there in huge numbers.

Rocky shores are encrusted with millions of barnacles, mussels, limpets, and other tough-shelled marine animals, which seal themselves up to sit out the few hours when the tide is out. Sandy shores may look empty, but the sand near the water line is full of buried shellfish, worms, sea urchins, and crabs, waiting for the tide to come back in again.

A coral reef teems with life off the coast of Indonesia. The fish and other animals feed on the plankton that rides the ocean currents.

Some of the most spectacular coastal habitats are *coral reefs*. They are created by corals, plantlike animals that are related to sea anemones. Corals live in colonies somewhat like flowering bushes: each "flower" is a separate coral, but they are all linked together. Reef-building corals make themselves tubes of chalky rock to live in, and over time, these rocky tubes build up to form a reef. Reefs are full of nooks and crannies that make ideal shelters from storms, tides, and enemies. Like the rainforests on land, coral reefs are simply bursting with life.

Fossils indicate that horseshoe crabs have been roaming beaches and shallow ocean waters for approximately 450 million years, making them one of the world's longest-living species. Their habitats and mating grounds are threatened by coastal development.

They are home to thousands of different kinds of fish, shellfish, and other animals.

Some animals do not have to wait for the tide to come in. Shore crabs scurry about on the open shore searching for dead fish and other delicacies. They have gills for breathing in water, but on land, they survive by carrying their own supplies of water for breathing, just as *scuba divers* carry their own air supply in tanks on their back. Their tight shells protect them from drying out. On tropical shores, ghost crabs and fiddler crabs survive in a similar way. They swarm in the thousands on food-rich beaches.

Some of the best feeding grounds are the mudflats in sheltered bays and river estuaries. When the tide is out, many different kinds of birds probe the mud for worms and other creatures buried below the surface.

In the tropics, mudflats also support trees called *mangroves*, which grow from tangles of roots sprouting from the mud. Underwater plants called *sea-grasses* also colonize sheltered mudflats, and in warm seas, green turtles and strange seal-like manatees and dugongs graze on the sea-grasses.

Life in the Mid-Ocean

Compared to the murky green waters often seen around coasts, the clear blue waters of mid-ocean look pure and unpolluted. Yet very little actually lives in these vast expanses of open ocean. They are like blue-water deserts.

One of the most famous is the Sargasso Sea. It lies in the middle of the North Atlantic, surrounded by a great swirl of ocean currents. These currents carry minerals that encourage plankton growth, but the minerals never reach the Sargasso Sea. As a result, there is no plankton and no fish, or very few. So the Sargasso Sea is literally the dead center of the ocean.

Life in the Deep Ocean

In the oceans, most of the action takes place within 660 feet (200m) of the surface. Yet large areas of the world's oceans are almost two miles deep. What lives in this huge volume of ocean water?

The answer is not a lot, compared with the teeming life up near the surface. Below 660 feet (200m), there is not enough light to support plants, so there is nothing to attract plankton-eating fish and their predators. But there is food. All the activ-

Glowing Fish

The hatchet fish lives in the deep ocean off the coast of California, Chile, and in the north Indian Ocean, where this three-inch (8cm) creature preys on shrimp (pictured here) while being hunted by larger fish.

Like many deep-water fish, the hatchet fish glows with an eerie blue light. This glow is not decorative, but protective. Most fish that live in shallower waters close to the coasts have silver bellies. This coloring matches the silver glitter of light on the surface, making the fish almost invisible to hunters from below. In the depths of the ocean, sunlight only produces a soft blue glow from above, so the hatchet fish generates a matching glow from rows of light-producing organs on its belly. This keeps the fish from appearing as a tempting black silhouette against the blue.

ity in the upper ocean creates a fallout of edible material, including dead plankton, scraps of meat, and even whole carcasses. It all sinks slowly into the black depths.

This "marine snow" of edible scraps is eaten by a variety of animals such as shrimp and jellyfish, which are preyed on in turn by deep-ocean fish and squid. Many of these glow in the dark, with a weird light produced by special cells called photophores.

These deep-ocean dwellers often have huge mouths bristling with long, needlelike teeth. The teeth ensure that scarce prey do not escape, and their huge mouths, combined with stomachs that expand like balloons, mean that they can eat animals much bigger than themselves. These killers look terrifying, but most are surprisingly small. They simply cannot get enough food to grow any bigger.

Yet there are monsters in the depths. The colossal sperm whale routinely dives to 3,300 feet (1,000m) or more, searching for its favorite prey, the giant squid. Squid can grow to 49 feet (15m) long, with eight arms and two long tentacles for catching fish. Giant squid have the biggest eyes in the whole animal kingdom. They are the size of dinner plates—up to 12 inches (30 centimeters) across. These huge eyes enable the squid to see its victims in the dim blue twilight 2,600 feet (800m) or so below the surface.

  Text-Dependent Questions

1. What is a food chain? What animal is at the bottom of the ocean food chain?
2. What part of the ocean is the richest of marine habitats?
3. What are some animals that live in the deep oceans?

  Research Project

Do some research on ocean plants, using your school library or the internet. What are some ways that these plants have adapted to survive? How do they spread their seeds, or protect themselves from being eaten? Write a two-page report and share your findings with the class.

 Words to Understand

fossil fuels—carbon-rich substances such as coal, oil, and natural gas which were formed by the deomposition of ancient plants and animals. The energy absorbed by the plants and animals in life is "fossilized," and released when the fuel is burned.

pollution—anything that spills into the air or water, and is not part of its natural chemistry. Includes both poisons and nutrient-rich fertilizers and sewage.

The wealth of Hong Kong originally came from its harbor, which lies on one of the great marine trade routes of the world.

3

The Benefits of Healthy Oceans

Humans use the world's oceans as highways, hunting grounds, and amusement parks. They are also rich sources of valuable fuels such as oil and gas. But as human populations grow and we use up resources on land, the oceans are coming under increasing pressure as we pollute them and overexploit their resources.

Two-thirds of the world's human population lives in coastal communities, because the oceans are rich sources of wealth. For centuries, oceans have provided a relatively easy way of transporting heavy loads and of trading with other countries. Many of the world's richest cities—places like New York, London, Tokyo, Hong Kong, Singapore, and Sydney—started life as seaports.

Food from the Oceans

Much of the wealth carried on ships comes from other coun-

A villager throws a fishing net near the village of Cochin, India. Small-scale fishing is important to many coastal communities around the world, and does little damage to fish stocks.

tries, but some is obtained from the oceans themselves. The most ancient of these ocean resources is food.

Fish and shellfish have been part of the human diet for thousands of years. At first, people just gathered shellfish from the shores, but the development of primitive boats, nets, hooks, and lines soon enabled them to catch fish. This kind of small-scale fishing is still practiced in coastal communities all over the world.

About a century ago, fishing became more scientific as the development of steam fishing boats allowed large fleets to target schools of fish wherever they were. Throughout the early twentieth century, fishing boats and their equipment became more efficient. Bigger and better engines meant that boats could follow the schools wherever they went.

One of the most important innovations has been the development of efficient onboard refrigeration systems, which allow the fish to be frozen as soon as they are caught. But frozen fish cannot be processed, so this then led to onboard fish processing, before the fish are loaded into the freezer. Fishing fleets with these facilities can stay at sea for weeks, and exploit fish stocks in remote oceans.

Commercial fishing techniques enable larger catches of fish, which can feed the world's growing population. However, overfishing of ocean waters can have a devastating effect on the marine ecosystem.

Large rigs are needed to access offshore reserves of oil and natural gas. While these fuels are important to the U.S. economy, extracting them pollutes the oceans and effects fish and wildlife in the biome.

Fish and shellfish are still among the most important ocean resources. Vast quantities are caught for sale in supermarkets—fresh, frozen, and canned—and more are caught for processing into fish meal, which is used for fertilizer and animal food.

Other Resources from Oceans

More than a third of the world's salt comes from the oceans. The production of salt is an ancient industry, especially in warm countries, since salt can be extracted from seawater by simply flooding a shallow pool and letting the water dry out under the sun. The white crystals left behind are sea salt. Sea salt is used to preserve and add flavor to food, and it contains minerals like potassium, calcium, zinc, and iron that are needed to keep the human body functioning properly.

Educational Video

For a video on the benefits of healthy oceans, scan here:

Ocean water contains many other minerals, including metals such as magnesium and even gold, but most of these exist in such small quantities that they are rarely worth the trouble of extracting from seawater.

Minerals under the seabed are another matter, however. About one-third of the world's total reserves of oil and natural gas lie under the shallow seas of the continental shelves. These *fossil fuels* are so valuable—both as fuel and as the raw material for plastics—that huge sums of money have been invested to extract them from beneath the waves. Roughly a quarter of the world's crude oil and about one-fifth of the world's natural gas are now produced by offshore drilling rigs.

The oceans can also provide other forms of power. Ocean winds, waves, and tides can all be harnessed to drive electricity generators. As governments become more concerned about the effects of human activity on climate change, these renewable power sources will become even more important in the future.

Offshore wind farms provide electricity with no pollution, unlike burning fossil fuels. They help to reduce the problem of global warming.

Enjoying the Oceans

All people use power, and most people eat fish, yet for many people the ocean means one thing—summer fun. Every year, millions of people head for the beach to enjoy the ocean. In many parts of the world, such as the Mediterranean Sea, tourism is the main local industry. Hotels, restaurants, and marinas have spread along the shore, and the coastal shallows are full of swimmers, sailors, and scuba divers.

It all seems like harmless fun, but the huge numbers of tourists—and the facilities provided for them—can have a surprisingly big impact on ocean wildlife. Other activities can be even more damaging, causing *pollution*, extinction, and even the destruction of whole ocean habitats.

Text-Dependent Questions

1. What percentage of the world's human population lives in coastal communities?
2. What innovations have allowed commercial fishing fleets to stay at sea for weeks and exploit fish stocks in remote oceans?

Research Project

Using your school library or the Internet, research some ways that people can derive electrical energy from the ocean, other than through the extraction of fossil fuels. Select one and find out more about it. Write a two-page report and share it with your class.

 Words to Understand

drift net—a fishing net that hangs in the water like a curtain, from floats at the surface.

erosion—the grinding away of rocks by natural forces such as ocean waves.

longline—a very long fishing line with thousands of baited hooks attached to it, used to catch fish such as tuna.

pesticides—poisonous chemicals used to kill weeds and insect pests, which drain into rivers and into the oceans.

purse seine—a fishing net that is set to encircle a school of fish and then closed off like a purse, so no fish can escape.

quota—a maximum number of fish (or other animals) that can be caught during a particular period.

salt marsh—a grassy swamp that develops on sheltered, salty mudflats in cool climates; the nontropical equivalent of a mangrove swamp.

trawl—a sock-shaped fishing net dragged across the seabed to catch fish that live on the bottom, such as flatfish and cod.

4

A humpback whale breaches, or leaps out of the water. Humpback whales were hunted to the brink of extinction. Although the humpback population has risen over the past five decades, the total population is still only about 80,000 whales.

How Humans Damage the Oceans

In the past, people have destroyed whole populations of marine animals. The great whales that once roamed the oceans in the thousands have been almost wiped out, and many are now very rare. Overfishing of fish such as cod, herring, and tuna could easily destroy these animals, too.

Destroying the Whale Population

On January 17, 1773, the ships *Adventure* and *Resolution*, commanded by Captain James Cook, became the first known ships to cross the Antarctic Circle. Heading south on a voyage of exploration, they discovered an icy world teeming with life. The bleak, rocky islands were alive with seals and penguins, and the stormy waters of the Southern Ocean heaved with great whales. Greatest of all were the blue whales, up to 98 feet (30m) long and weighing up to 150 metric tons—the biggest animals that have ever lived.

By the late 1700s, seal and whale hunters in northern oceans were already running short of prey. Following Cook's lead, they headed south, and began one of the greatest mass slaughters in history. The fur seals were the first to suffer, clubbed to death for their pelts. A typical sealing ship might take up to 9,000 seals in just three weeks, and there were hundreds of such ships. By the 1830s, there were virtually no fur seals left, so the hunters switched to killing whales for their valuable oil.

Harpooning whales was a lot more difficult and dangerous than clubbing seals, but the invention of the explosive harpoon

Seagulls eat pilot whale carcasses in the Faroe Islands. The native islanders slaughter about 800 pilot whales each summer when they swim close to the islands, and butcher them for meat and oil.

The Japanese government still allows an annual whale hunt, which it claims is for the purpose of learning more about whale populations; however, Japanese "research ships" like this one kill over 300 whales each season and bring the meat back to Japan, where it is regarded as a delicacy. The Japanese hunts have been condemned by the International Whaling Commission and many other nations and international organizations.

in 1864 enabled the whalers to kill virtually every whale they saw. By 1930, they were killing 30,000 blue whales a year. As the blue whales became scarce, they turned to right whales, humpbacks, and others. Before long, the whales were nearly all gone.

As whale populations dwindled, maximum catch numbers, or *quotas*, were agreed upon by various nations to control the hunting of whales. The quotas were set by the International Whaling Commission (IWC), which was set up for this purpose in 1946. But the quotas were often too high, and whale populations continued to fall. Eventually, pressure from the United Nations forced a total ban on commercial whaling in 1985. Although some countries still practice "scientific" whaling, whale numbers are gradually increasing.

An Overfishing Crisis

The story of whaling is the most dramatic example of ocean wildlife destruction, but today many types of fish are suffering from depletion almost as badly as the whales were in the early twentieth century. Modern technology such as electronic depth sounders or fishfinders helps fishing boats to accurately locate schools of fish, such as herring and tuna. They can then encircle the fish with a *purse seine*—a type of net that can be closed off at the bottom like a string bag—and scoop the entire school from the water. This technique virtually wiped out the herring stocks in the northeast Atlantic, and in 1976, herring fishing was banned in this region. Many tuna stocks have also fallen.

In contrast to such focused fishing, other fishing fleets use nets that catch virtually anything in their path. *Trawl* nets, for instance, are hauled across the seabed to catch fish such as hake, cod, and haddock. The trawls act like underwater bulldozers, killing and injuring many more animals than they catch. They also take so many fish that hake and cod populations in European waters are

Educational Video

For a short video on the problem of overfishing, scan here:

A commercial fishing boat with a purse seine net staged for a fishing trip. In a single haul, a purse seine can net an entire school of fish, with a devastating effect on ocean fish stocks.

now at dangerously low levels. Quotas have been imposed, but as with the whaling quotas, the permitted catches are too high, so fish stocks are still declining.

Since 1989, when about 90 million metric tons of fish were taken from the ocean worldwide, the amount of fish caught each year has declined. As of 2018, 80 percent of commercial fish stocks are considered "fully exploited" or "overexploited." Fisheries for the most sought-after species, like orange roughy, Chilean sea bass, and bluefin tuna have collapsed. A recent scientific report estimated that industrial fishing has reduced the number of large ocean fish to just 10 percent of their pre-industrial population.

Due to the collapse of large-fish populations, commercial fleets are going deeper in the ocean and father down the food chain for viable catches. This so-called "fishing down" is triggering a chain reaction that is upsetting the ancient and delicate balance of the sea's biologic system. A recent study published in the journal *Science* predicted that if the current fishing rates continue, all the world's fisheries will collapse by the year 2048.

How Overfishing Affects Other Marine Animals

Fish are the main food of many marine animals, so if the fish disappear, these animals have nothing to eat. Seabirds such as puffins depend upon small fish such as sand eels and capelin to feed their young. But these fish have become profitable to catch, and the fishing fleets scoop so many from the north Atlantic that several breeding colonies of puffins have vanished altogether. Seabirds can also become tangled in fishing nets and drown.

During the 1980s, huge *drift nets* several miles long were developed to catch tuna and squid in the Pacific. Known as "wall of death" nets, these snared any ocean animals that ran into them, including diving seabirds, seals, dolphins, and turtles. One fishing trip by a fleet of 32 Japanese drift-netting boats resulted in the death of over 1,000 small whales, 52 seals, 22 turtles, and over 50,000 sharks. Such death rates led to these kinds of nets being banned in 1993, although enforcing the ban has not been easy. Manufacturers have modified the nets so that they fall into the legal guidelines, but still can take in huge amounts of fish. And fishing with illegal nets is common in international waters.

Another method of fishing involves attaching up to 20,000 baited hooks to a line up to 75 miles (120 km) long, and trailing it through the water. This *longlining* technique has become popular with tuna boats. Unfortunately, longlining doesn't just catch tuna. Seabirds and sea turtles try to snatch the bait from the line before it sinks, and inevitably, some are hooked in the bill or throat and drown.

Protecting Fisheries and Birds

Perhaps the best-known accidental victims of fishing are dolphins. They often hunt in partnership with tuna, and the tuna fleets discovered that encircling a dolphin school with a purse seine was a sure way of netting a school of tuna. But the dolphins were netted, too. Unlike tuna, dolphins are mammals that need to breathe air, so when trapped in a net they often

Many sea turtles are snared in discarded fishing nets when they dive to catch fish. Unable to maneuver properly, they can drown or become easy targets for predators.

drowned. When this became widely known, there was a public outcry, and the tuna fleets were forced to employ divers that would open panels in the nets to release the dolphins before they became fatally entangled. Tuna caught in this way—or by using poles and lines instead of nets—is labelled "dolphin friendly." Yet the problem has not gone away, and many of the early "dolphin friendly" tuna nets still snared a lot of dolphins.

There are ways of preventing the accidental capture of seabirds by longlining boats. Some of the main victims of longlining capture are albatrosses. These magnificent birds spend most of their lives in the air, soaring over the Southern

Ocean. But they often follow ships, including longlining fishing boats, and since they feed on fish and squid, they are easily attracted to baited lines, and are hooked and dragged under. Setting the hooks at night, weighting the lines, and using bird scarers all help stop accidental bird capture. These measures are now enforced by law, and as a result, the legitimate longliners have reduced their total seabird catch by an amazing 90 percent. But many longlining boats operating in the Southern Ocean are illegal, and these "pirates" still kill up to 100,000 seabirds each year, including around 20,000 albatrosses.

In recent years there have been many modifications to fishing gear so that non-target species can escape, or are not caught in the first place. Often, these modifications are simple and inexpensive, and they are often suggested by the fishermen themselves.

Poisoning the Water

Every year, vast quantities of waste are deliberately or accidentally dumped in the oceans. This waste includes dangerous chemicals, oil, and sewage, as well as huge amounts of garbage. Coastal communities produce about 700 million tons of solid sewage per year. The pollution threatens to poison the water of oceans and shallow seas, destroying their wildlife.

In the early twenty-first century, a routine check on marine life in the Severn estuary in western Britain discovered that the fish living there were radioactive. Their bodies contained tritium, which is a product of nuclear power plants. These plants pump millions of gallons of tritium-contaminated waste water into the ocean every year, in the belief that it will disperse and then disappear. But the tritium levels found in the fish show otherwise.

The Severn estuary is not the only example of this—there are thousands of others around the world every year. In 2017, for example, the company that was cleaning up a badly damaged nuclear reactor in Fukushima, Japan, announced plans to release hundreds of thousands of metric tons of highly radioactive water into the Pacific Ocean. The highly controversial plan was supported by the Japanese government, although it was opposed by many scientists and activists around the world.

Garbage Dumping and Oil Spills

For centuries, people have used the oceans as dumping grounds for our garbage. Pipelines from coastal towns carry raw sewage and waste from factories out beyond the tide line and into the water. Garbage is routinely thrown overboard from ships. For years, oil tankers have cleaned out their tanks at sea, flushing waste oil into the oceans. Bales of domestic waste, drums of toxic chemical waste, and even sealed containers of nuclear waste are taken out to sea and dumped. Much of this activity is illegal, but it happens anyway because dumping from ships is difficult to stop.

This deliberate pollution of the oceans is just part of the problem. Huge quantities of fertilizers, *pesticides*, and other agricultural chemicals drain off the land, into rivers, and out to sea. Silt and sludge from mines and quarries also end up in the ocean. As much as 40 percent of all ocean pollution comes from the land in this way. Meanwhile, offshore drilling for oil pollutes the water with oil-contaminated mud, and every day,

Garbage, much of it plastic, washed ashore on an otherwise pristine beach. It is estimated that 8 million metric tons of waste plastic end up in the oceans each year. Sea creatures ingest plastic particles, and people in turn eat the contaminated fish and shellfish.

fishing boats lose nets that drift in the ocean for years, trapping and killing marine wildlife.

Oil floats on water, causing great oil slicks that drift with the winds and currents. They can be broken up with detergents somewhat like dishwashing liquid, but this just makes a toxic sludge that sinks to the seabed. If the oil slick blows onshore, it smothers and poisons the coast, and in remote areas with rich wildlife, the effects can be catastrophic.

The effects of pollution are worst in small seas, since the pollutants are not washed away into the vastness of the ocean. The North Sea, for example, is badly polluted with oil from drilling platforms, industrial waste, and pesticides, and the

A worker helps clean up an oil spill on the beach at Koh Samet, a popular resort in Thailand. The spill occurred in 2013 when an offshore pipeline broke off the coast.

Baltic Sea is even worse. The poisons in the water affect fish, seabirds, and seals, making them prone to disease.

In 2010, an offshore oil rig called Deepwater Horizon that was operating in the Gulf of Mexico experienced a blowout and explosion that led to the worst oil spill in U.S. waters, and one of the worst marine oil spills in history. According to the U.S. government, between April and July 2010 approximately 4.9 million barrels (210 million U.S. gallons) spilled into the Gulf. A massive effort was coordinated to try to prevent the oil from reaching the beaches and wetlands of Louisiana, Mississippi, Alabama, Texas, Florida and other Gulf states. Ultimately, about 500 miles (800 km) of coastline was contaminated by the massive oil spill, resulting in billions of dollars in cleanup costs, as well as untold damage to fish, seabirds, and other marine life. The ecological damage from the spill is still being determined.

In the Mediterranean, one of the main threats to wildlife is pollution by raw sewage. At least 80 percent of the 500 million metric tons of sewage dumped in the Mediterranean every year is untreated. Besides the disease risk, this also works a bit like throwing fertilizer into the sea. It makes the plankton grow much faster than usual, causing "blooms" of microscopic plants. Some of the planktonic plants that grow in sewage-polluted waters can release poisons that kill fish and other animals, and when the plankton bloom dies, it creates a foul, decaying sludge that uses up all the oxygen in the water.

There are laws against deliberately polluting the oceans. They may be hard to enforce, but they are having some effect. The amount of oil pollution from shipping, for example, has gone down since the 1970s. Many accidents can be prevented through improved technology. Problems such as raw sewage are harder to deal with, because many coastal communities cannot pay for proper sewage processing.

Damage on the Coasts

In the summer, many people head for the coast to enjoy the beach and the water. But the hotels and other developments that are built to cater for tourists—and earn money for local people—are turning wild coastlines into coastal towns. They are also threatening to destroy the marine wildlife that many of the tourists come to see.

The power of the ocean is most obvious on the world's coasts. Great waves crash into cliffs, grinding them away through *erosion* and carrying off the pieces to build beaches from shingle and sand. The spectacular coastal landscapes created by these processes attract millions of tourists.

Yet the tourists that visit coasts are destroying many of the most fragile coastal habitats. The money to be made from tourism encourages the construction of hotels all along the shore, and these have to be protected by sea walls. The natural shoreline is sealed beneath concrete, and the whole system of erosion and beach building is upset.

Meanwhile, much of the plant life along the shore is stripped away. This may include *salt marshes* and tropical mangrove swamps, both rich habitats for marine animals. When plant life along the shore is stripped away, bare soil is washed into the ocean.

Coral reefs are particularly vulnerable to the washing of soil from land into the ocean, because corals need clear, sunlit water to survive. Large areas of coral have been destroyed like this in the Caribbean. Sea-grass beds—vital food sources for manatees and dugongs—can be smothered in the same way. They may also be scoured away by changes in the flow of the tides, or destroyed by dredging for building sand.

Other victims of coastal development include sea turtles, which emerge from the sea to bury their eggs on deserted beaches. Each species of turtle uses the same beaches each year. Kemp's Ridley turtle, one of the rarest, uses just a few sites on a 12 mile (20 km) stretch of beach in Mexico. Conservation organizations such as World Wildlife Fund (WWF) have had some success in protecting Kemp's Ridley turtle, but if the nesting beaches of this or other turtle species are destroyed, the turtles will probably disappear completely.

The development of coastal areas can result in greater damage when storms hit. In October 2012 a powerful storm called Hurricane Sandy hit the northeastern United States. In many shore towns, where houses and hotels had been built where the sand dunes once stood, the storm caused great damage and flooding. In stretches of beachfront where the sand dunes and the grasses that held them in place remained, the damage was less severe. Overall, Hurricane Sandy caused approximately $75 billion in damage.

Marine Reserves

Some coastal waters have been declared "marine reserves." All fishing is outlawed, along with any other damaging activity. But enforcing the law is not easy. The waters around Cocos Island off Costa Rica, for example, have been declared a fully protected World Heritage Site. Yet every night, they are invaded by illegal shark fishing boats. These lay longlines up to 30 miles (50km) long, which catch thousands of sharks each month, as well as turtles, dolphins, and swordfish. There are not enough rangers to police the reserves properly, and the rich marine life of the island may be destroyed.

Tourism is also causing problems. Thousands of visitors to coastal resorts may spend their time sailing, waterskiing, fishing, or scuba diving. These activities may seem harmless, but they mean trouble for coastal wildlife. Boat propellers injure marine mammals such as dolphins, manatees, and seals. Sea

Native trees and plants that anchor protective sand dunes are often swept away to make room for coastal development, such as this resort town on the coast of Spain.

angling and spear fishing can threaten rare fish. The collection of reef specimens by scuba divers has damaged many coral reefs, and boat anchors often tear up big chunks of coral.

At the end of each day, the tourists want to eat local food. At many beach resorts this means fish, and the demand may be met by drastic methods. On the reefs off the Philippines, fish are caught illegally by tossing dynamite into the water. The explosion kills or injures every animal within range—not just the edible fish—and shatters the coral. Reef fish are also caught for exhibition in local aquariums, using cyanide (a deadly poison) to stun the fish in the water—a technique that kills far more than it catches. Raw sewage from coastal resorts is often dumped in the sea, and this adds to the destruction.

Some tourists help preserve natural coastal environments. This is because they are willing to pay higher prices than normal to stay on coasts that do not have buildings like high-rise hotels, and are still rich in wildlife. The extra amount of money that these "ecotourists" pay means that local people can make a good living without overdeveloping the coastline. This approach has been adopted on the Australian Great Barrier Reef, which is the world's largest coral reef system. Yet even here, the sheer number of visitors threatens the reefs.

Text-Dependent Questions

1. In what year was the International Whaling Commission established?
2. What is the difference between fishing with drift nets and longlining?
3. What effect to oil spills and illegal garbage dumping have on oceans and coastal areas.
4. How do coastal development and tourism affect the ocean in negative ways? What are the positive effects?

Research Project

The 2010 Deepwater Horizons oil spill was one of many devastating spills over the years. Other notable oil spills included the failure of the oil rig Ixtoc 1 in 1979, or the crashes of oil tankers *Amoco Cadiz* (1978) and *Exxon Valdez* (1989). Using your school library or the internet, search for oil spills and the ocean and choose one event. How did the spill occur? How was it stopped or contained? What were the ecological effects? Write a two-page report with your findings, and share it with your class.

 Words to Understand

atmosphere—the blanket of gas that envelops the Earth. It is mostly nitrogen and oxygen, with small amounts of carbon dioxide and other gases.

ice age—a period of cooler temperatures, when glaciers covered the earth.

The polar bear is becoming a casualty of global warming, because its sea ice habitat is melting beneath its feet.

Climate Change and the World's Oceans

The world's climate is always changing. Slow, natural cycles bring worldwide *ice ages* and warm periods that can last for thousands or millions of years. But over the last century human activity has caused a relatively rapid warming that could have dramatic effects on the oceans and on the people who live near them.

Increasing Pace of Change

The global climate has always changed very slowly, but now it is changing much faster. The change may not seem fast by human standards: in Alaska, average temperatures have risen by almost 2° Fahrenheit per decade over the past thirty years. But this is a lot faster than any natural cycle of climate change. And as far as scientists can tell, the root cause is pollution of the *atmosphere*.

The atmosphere doesn't just provide the air we breathe. It

Catastrophic storms like Hurricane Sandy, which devastated coastal towns in New York and New Jersey in 2012, could become more frequent as the climate changes.

also protects us from the most dangerous of the Sun's rays and acts something like the glass of a greenhouse, letting light in by day but keeping heat in at night. The "glass" is really a mixture of gases, including carbon dioxide, which are particularly good at keeping the heat in. So the more "greenhouse gas" that there is in the atmosphere, the warmer the Earth gets.

Educational Video

Scan here for a short animated video on rising sea levels:

Scientists analyzing air bubbles preserved in ancient polar ice have discovered that the amount of carbon dioxide in the atmosphere has risen steadily over the past 150 years. The increase almost exactly matches the rise in global temperature. So it seems that rising carbon dioxide levels are the main cause of global warming. Most of the extra carbon dioxide is being released by burning carbon-rich fossil fuels such as coal, oil, gasoline, and natural gas. These are used in electricity generating stations, car engines, and home heating. So the more power we use, the worse it gets.

The Effect on the Oceans

When water heats up, it expands to take up more space. So as the world gets warmer, polar ice melts and sea levels rise. They have already risen by 4 to 8 inches (10 to 20 cm) since 1900, and are currently predicted to rise by up to 42 inches (107 cm) by the year 2100. As sea levels continue to rise, flooding will

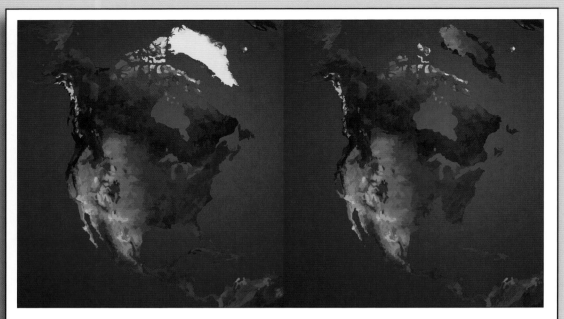

As sea levels rise, they will flood low-lying areas. This illustration shows the current coastline of North America (left), as well as what the continent could look like after severe warming has melted the Arctic ice cap (right).

become routine, and many coastal communities could be swept away.

Things could—and likely will—get even worse. Immense volumes of water are locked up in the ice sheets that cover Greenland and Antarctica. Satellite data has shown that these are melting at an ever-increasing rate. From 2004 to 2014, the Greenland ice sheet has lost an average of 303 billion metric tons of ice every year, while the Antarctic has lost, on average, 118 billion metric tons of ice annually. Because the edges of the ice sheet float on water, warming currents have increased the melting rate. Once these floating ice sheets are gone, the glaciers will melt even faster.

Ice acts like a mirror, reflecting light back into space, so if there is less ice, the planet will absorb more light and more heat. Eventually, there could be a runaway thaw, and all the meltwater would cascade into the oceans.

If the Greenland ice sheet melts completely, it would cause a sea-level rise of up to 20 feet (6m). If the Antarctice ice sheet melts, it would cause sea levels to rise 164 feet (50m). Long before this happens, coral islands like the Maldives would disappear, low-lying countries such as Bangladesh would become

As global temperatures rise, so do sea levels, causing regular flooding in low-lying regions of Asia and the Pacific. Sixty-five percent of cities with populations of more than 2.5 million are located on coasts. Many are at or below the present sea level, so they are threatened by sea-level rise due to climate change.

shallow seas, and major coastal cities throughout the world such as New York and Miami would be swamped. Since two-thirds of the world's population lives in coastal communities, most people would be flooded out.

Other Problems

The warm Gulf Stream that gives Europe its mild climate is powered by ice that forms during the winter months on the fringes of the Arctic Ocean. This makes the salty water flowing north colder and even saltier, so it sinks and flows south along the ocean floor. As it sinks, it draws warm surface water north to take its place. But satellite and submarine measurements have found that over the past twenty years less ice forms in the western Arctic during the winter months each year, and more is lost during the summer months. As ocean temperatures rise, the water may stop sinking, which would affect the Gulf Stream, which warms Europe. In this scenario, Europe could become as cold as Labrador in eastern Canada. Studies indicate the Gulf Stream has slowed over the past twenty years by 15 to 20 percent.

Tropical currents are also being affected right now. El Niño, which affects the weather in the eastern Pacific, is caused when warmer water pushes cold currents to the south. Strong El Niño events are happening more often, and becoming more severe, and scientists believe these are linked to global warming. At some point, the oceans may experience strong El Niño events every year, along with all the powerful storms, floods, and droughts that they cause in the tropics. The rest of the world will suffer the fallout from these extreme weather patterns, and our weather could become even less predictable than it is now.

What Lies Ahead?

The oceans are huge, but they are not limitless. Humans have discovered this the hard way, as fish become scarce and marine habitats such as coral reefs are damaged. But if people act

Manhattan may seem a long way from the Maldives, but the pollution released by all these cars helps cause the global warming that is killing the world's coral reefs.

responsibly, they can help the oceans recover to full health, and maybe give ourselves a more secure future.

Much of the ocean floor has never been explored, and probably never will be. It is an alien world, more mysterious than the surface of the Moon. The vastness and mystery of the oceans has encouraged us to treat them as if they had no limits. For centuries, we have fished them for food, and put nothing back except our garbage. And up to a point, the oceans can cope. Surviving fish eventually breed and produce more fish. Garbage such as sewage and oil eventually breaks down and becomes harmless. It is even possible that the plankton in the oceans may multiply to absorb much of the extra carbon dioxide that humans are pumping into the atmosphere.

But meanwhile, things are going wrong. Many fish are becoming scarce. Pollution is damaging coastlines. Ocean currents and weather systems are changing as global temperatures rise, causing more storms, flooding, and droughts. Rising sea temperatures are killing the world's coral reefs. Things look bad for the ocean biome, and they could get worse.

There are plenty of things that people can do to help to protect the world's oceans and reverse the damage that humans have caused. We can eat a wider variety of fish, and fewer of the species that are getting scarce. We can reject tuna caught using methods that harm dolphins and other ocean life. When we visit the coast, we can avoid activities that damage marine habitats such as coral reefs, and stop buying souvenirs made from coral, seashells, and turtle shell.

Yet the main reason why the oceans have gotten into this state is that there are too many people using too much energy and dumping too much garbage. A typical American, for example, uses three times more materials and energy than the global average, and the U.S. produces more than a third of the world's carbon dioxide. If we all threw less away, turned down the thermostat or air conditioning and made fewer car trips, it would have a big impact on pollution and global warming. It might make all the difference for the future of the oceans.

 ## Text-Dependent Questions

1. What is climate change? What do scientists believe is the root cause?
2. How much would sea levels rise if the Antarctic ice sheet melts?
3. What would be the effect if the Gulf Stream slows or stops flowing?

 ## Research Project

Using your school library or the internet, do some research to answer the question, "Should we cut greenhouse gas emissions?" Most scientists support the 1997 Kyoto Protocol, which calls upon each nation to cut its emissions of carbon dioxide and other greenhouse gases by about 7 percent. This, they hope, would slow down the rate of climate change. However, opponents of the treaty argue that cutting emissions by 7 percent would make little difference to global warming, but would mean drastic cutbacks in industry, putting many Americans out of work. Write a two-page report, using data and examples to support your conclusion.

Quick Reference

Oceans

The world's oceans cover an area of 139 million square miles (361 million sq km)—about 71 percent of the world's surface. About 80 percent of the ocean is more than 1 mile (3km) deep. There are five major oceans:

Pacific Ocean: 60,060,700 sq mi (155,557,000 sq km)
Atlantic Ocean: 29,637,900 sq mi (76,762,000 sq km)
Indian Ocean: 26,469,900 sq mi (68,566,000 sq km)
Southern Ocean: 7,848,300 sq mi (20,327,000 sq km)
Arctic Ocean: 5,427,000 sq mi (14,056,000 sq km)

People use the terms "ocean" and "sea" interchangeably when speaking about the ocean. However, seas are smaller and shallower than oceans, and are often part of a larger ocean. The world's largest seas include:

Mediterranean Sea: 1,144,800 sq mi (2,965,018 sq km)
Caribbean Sea: 1,049,500 square miles (2,718,193 sq km)
South China Sea: 895,400 square miles (2,319,075 sq km)
Bering Sea: 884,900 square miles (2,291,880 sq km)
Gulf of Mexico: 615,000 square miles (1,592,843 sq km)
Okhotsk Sea: 613,800 square miles (1,589,735 sq km)

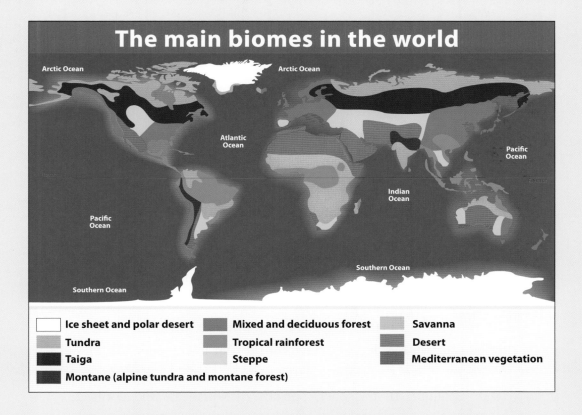

The main biomes in the world

Arctic Ocean
Arctic Ocean
Atlantic Ocean
Pacific Ocean
Indian Ocean
Pacific Ocean
Southern Ocean
Southern Ocean

Ice sheet and polar desert
Tundra
Taiga
Montane (alpine tundra and montane forest)
Mixed and deciduous forest
Tropical rainforest
Steppe
Savanna
Desert
Mediterranean vegetation

The oceans can be divided into zones, according to depth. The photic zone (where light can reach) is from 0 to 660 feet (0 to 200m). The twilight zone is from 660 to 3,300 feet (200 to 1,000m). On average, the ocean floor is 12,240ft (3,730m) deep, although some areas are almost 7 miles (11km) deep.

The largest sea animal is the blue whale. It can be 108 feet (33m) long and weigh 150 tons. The longest animal is a siphonophore (an animal related to jellyfish) that grows to 130 feet (40m). The richest coral reefs are home to more than 700 species of coral, 5,000 species of mollusks, and 2,000 species of fish. Ninety percent of the world's fish live in coastal waters, and there is 1,000 times more life in the ocean shallows than on the deep ocean floor.

Climate Change

The Earth's climate has changed throughout history. During the last 650,000 years there have been seven cycles of glacial advance and retreat. The end of the last ice age, about 11,700 years ago, marks the beginning of the modern climate era—and of human civilization.

Today, the Earth is experiencing another warming period. Since the 1950s scientists have found that average global temperatures have gradually risen by more than 1° Fahrenheit (0.6° Celsius). In the past, periods of warming and cooling have been attributed to very small variations in Earth's orbit that change the amount of solar energy our planet receives. Two things make the current warming trend unusual. First, most scientists agree that the warming is probably caused by human activities that release carbon dioxide into the atmosphere. Second, the speed at which the Earth's temperature is rising is much faster than this phenomenon has ever occurred in the past, according to climate records.

The heat-trapping nature of carbon dioxide and other "greenhouse gases" was demonstrated in the mid-19th century. Without the Earth's atmosphere, the sun's energy would be reflected back into space. Greenhouse gases in the atmosphere trap some of the sun's heat, reflecting it back to keep the earth's

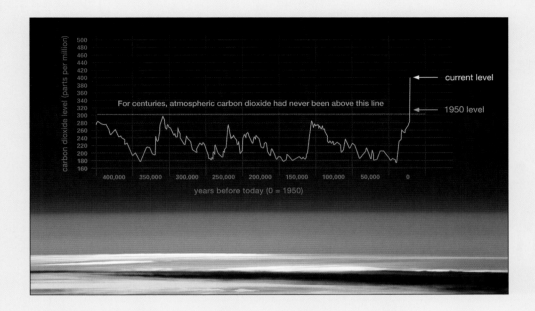

surface warmer than it would otherwise be. Without the atmosphere, the Earth's average temperature would be 0°F (–18°C). Thanks to the greenhouse effect, Earth's average temperature is currently about 59°F (15°C).

Increased levels of greenhouse gases in the atmosphere must cause the Earth to warm in response. Since the start of the Industrial Revolution in the mid-eighteenth century, human activities—including the burning of "fossil fuels" like oil, coal, and natural gas, as well as farming and the clearing of large forested areas—have produced a 40 percent increase in the atmospheric concentration of carbon dioxide, from 280 parts per million (ppm) in 1750 to over 400 ppm today.

Scientists understand how the Earth's climate has changed over the past 650,000 years by studying ice cores drawn from Greenland, Antarctica, and tropical mountain glaciers. Varying

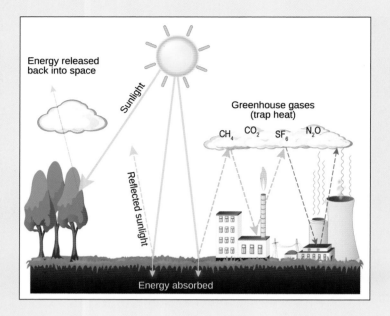

carbon dioxide levels found in the ancient ice show how the Earth's climate responds to changes in greenhouse gas levels. Ancient evidence can also be found in tree rings, ocean sediments, coral reefs, and layers of sedimentary rocks. This ancient, or paleoclimate, evidence reveals that current warming is occurring roughly ten times faster than the average rate of ice-age-recovery warming.

Most scientists believe that if greenhouse gas emissions continue at the present rate, Earth's surface temperature could grow much warmer than it has been in more than 650,000 years. Recent studies indicate that, if emissions are not reduced, the Earth could warm by another 3.6°F (2°C) over the next twenty years. This would have an extremely harmful effect on ecosystems, biodiversity, and the livelihoods of people worldwide.

Evidence of Climate Change

Earth's average surface temperature has risen about 2°F (1.1°C) since the late nineteenth century. Most of this warming has occurred over the past 35 years. Seventeen of the eighteen warmest years in recorded history have occurred since 2001, and 2017 was the warmest year on record.

Oceans have absorbed much of the increased heat, with the top 2,300 feet (700 meters) of ocean warming by 0.3°F since 1969.

The Greenland and Antarctic ice sheets have melted greatly over the past thirty years. Further melting of the ice sheets could result in significant rise in sea levels.

The strength and frequency of hurricanes and other extreme storms has risen along with global temperatures.

Series Glossary

atmosphere—an envelope of gases that surrounds the earth (or another planet). Earth's atmosphere, which is composed of mostly nitrogen and oxygen, helps the earth retain heat and reflect ultraviolet radiation.

biodiversity—the variety among and within plant and animal species in a particular environment.

biomass—the total of all living organisms in a given area.

biome—a very large ecological area, with plants and animals that are adapted to the environmental conditions there. Biomes are usually defined by their physical characteristics—such as climate, geology, or vegetation—rather than by the animals that live there.

climate—the long-term average weather pattern in a particular place.

climate change—a change in global or regional climate patterns. This term is generally used to refer to changes that have become apparent since the mid- to late-twentieth century that are attributed in large part to the increased levels of atmospheric carbon dioxide produced by the use of fossil fuels.

ecology—the scientific study of animals and plants in their natural surroundings.

ecosystem—all the living things, from plants and animals to microscopic organisms, that share and interact within a particular area.

food chain—a group of organisms interrelated by the fact that each member of the group feeds upon the one below it.

genus—a group of closely related species.

geodiversity—the variety of earth materials (such as minerals, rocks, or sediments) and processes (such as erosion or volcanic activity) that constitute and shape the Earth.

global warming—a gradual increase in the overall temperature of the earth's atmosphere. It is generally attributed to the greenhouse effect, caused by increased levels of carbon dioxide, chlorofluorocarbons, and other pollutants in the atmosphere.

greenhouse effect—a term used to describe warming of the atmosphere owing to the presence of carbon dioxide and other gases. Without the presence of these gases, heat from the sun would return to space in the form of infrared radiation. Carbon dioxide and other gases absorb some of this radiation and prevent its release, thereby warming the earth.

habitat—the natural home of a particular plant or animal species.

invasive species—a non-native species that, when introduced to an area, is likely to cause economic or environmental damage or harm to human health.

nutrient—chemical elements and compounds that provide organisms with the necessary nourishment.

species—a group of similar animals or plants that can breed together naturally and produce normal offspring.

umbrella species—a species selected for making conservation-related decisions, because protecting these species indirectly protects many other species that make up the ecological community of its habitat.

vegetation—ground cover provided by plants.

watershed—the land where water from rain and melted snow drains downhill into a body of water, such as a river, lake, reservoir, estuary, wetland, sea, or ocean.

Series Glossary

Further Reading

Earle, Sylvia A. *Blue Hope: Exploring and Caring for Earth's Magnificent Ocean*. Washington, D.C.: National Geographic, 2014.

Kalman, Bobbie. *The Ocean Biome*. New York: Crabtree Publishing, 2014.

Joppa, Lucas N., Jonathan E.M. Bailie, and John G. Robinson, eds. *Protected Areas: Are They Safeguarding Biodiversity?* Hoboken, N.J.: John Wiley and Sons, Ltd., 2016.

Kareiva, Peter, and Michelle Marvier. *Conservation Science: Balancing the Needs of People and Nature*. 2nd ed. New York: W.H. Freeman, 2014.

Kolbert, Elizabeth. *The Sixth Extinction: An Unnatural History*. New York: Henry Holt and Co., 2014.

Lindeen, Carol K. *Life in an Ocean*. North Mankato, Minn.: Capstone Press, 2016.

Taylor, Dorceta E. *The Rise of the American Conservation Movement: Power, Privilege, and Environmental Protection*. Durham, N.C.: Duke University Press, 2016.

Internet Resources

www.worldwildlife.org
The World Wildlife Fund (WWF) was founded in 1961 as an international fundraising organization, which works in collaboration with conservation groups to protect animals and their natural habitats.

www.audubon.org
The National Audubon Society is one of the oldest conservation organizations. It uses science, education, and grassroots advocacy to protect birds and their habitats around the world.

www.iucn.org
The International Union for Conservation of Nature (IUCN) includes both government and non-governmental organizations. It works to provide knowledge and tools so that economic development and nature conservation can take place together.

http://www.nwf.org
The National Wildlife Federation is the largest grassroots conservation organization in the United States, with over 6 million supporters and affiliated organizations in every state.

Publisher's Note: The websites listed on this page were active at the time of publication. The publisher is not responsible for websites that have changed their address or discontinued operation since the date of publication. The publisher reviews and updates the websites each time the book is reprinted.

www.fws.gov

The U.S. Fish and Wildlife Service is a branch of the government that is responsible for enforcing federal wildlife laws, protecting endangered species, and conserving and restoring wildlife habitats within the United States.

www.nmfs.noaa.gov

NOAA Fisheries is responsible for the stewardship of the nation's ocean resources, including the recovery and conservation of protected water habitats to promote healthy ecosystems.

www.nature.org

The Nature Conservancy is a leading conservation organization. It works in more than 70 countries to protect ecologically important lands and waters all over the world.

www.sierraclub.org

Founded by legendary conservationist John Muir in 1892, the Sierra Club is among the largest and most influential environmental organizations in the United States. The organization has protected millions of acres of wilderness, and helped to pass the Clean Air Act, Clean Water Act, and Endangered Species Act.

http://www.greenpeace.org

Greenpeace uses protests and creative communication to expose global environmental problems and promote solutions that are essential to a green and peaceful future.

Index

Numbers in ***bold italic*** refer to captions.

About the Author

Kimberly Sidabras is a freelance writer and editor. She worked with the World Wildlife Federation for nearly two decades. A graduate of Temple University, she lives near Philadelphia with her husband and three children. She is the author of five volumes in the WORLD'S BIOMES series (Mason Crest, 2019).